Primary Ecology Series

I Am a Part of Nature

Bobbie Kalman & Janine Schaub

Crabtree Publishing Company

Toronto · Oxford · New York

The Primary Ecology Series

To Uwe Schaub

Writing team
Bobbie Kalman
Janine Schaub

Editor-in-chief
Bobbie Kalman

Editors
Janine Schaub
Shelagh Wallace

Design and computer layout
Antoinette "Cookie" DeBiasi

Type output
Lincoln Graphics

Color separations
ISCOA

Printer
Lake Book Manufacturing

Illustrations
Antoinette "Cookie" DeBiasi: cover,
pages 15, 17; Karen Harrison: pages 7,
29, 30; Maureen Shaughnessy: page 19;
Barb Bedell: pages 8-11

Photographs
Sherman Hines/Masterfile: front cover
Peter Crabtree: pages 5 (bottom), 29
Ken Faris: page 28
Marc Crabtree: pages 5 (top), 6 (left)
Andre Baude: pages 6 (top and bottom right)
Greg Robinson: page 26 (right)
Diane Majumdar: title page, pages 4 (both), 12 (top),
14 (both), 16, 20 (bottom), page 21 (bottom), 24-25 (all 6)
Nature Interpretive Center at Royal Botanical Gardens:
page 27 (all 3)
Dave Taylor: page 23 (top)
Bobbie Kalman: back cover, pages 12, 13, 17, 18 (all 4),
20 (top), 21 (top), 22 (both), 23 (bottom), 26 (left), page 31
Crabtree Publishing Company made every attempt to
secure model releases.

"I am a part of nature" (pages 8-11) and **"The forest
recycling game"** (page 13) were written by Chris Taylor.

Special thanks to: The students of St. Clare School and
Jody Forsyth, their librarian; Marc Crabtree (who appears
on page 5), Heather Brissenden (on back cover), Olivia
Baude and her family on pages 6, 31; Steve Bowen at
RBG Nature Interpretive Center; Norma Paterson; the
students of Elmlea Junior School and Parliament Oak
Elementary School; Jackie Stafford; Maureen
Shaughnessy; Sam and Elvira Graci and my meditation
group who inspired this book

Published by
Crabtree Publishing Company

350 Fifth Ave.	360 York Road, R.R.4	73 Lime Walk
Suite 3308	Niagara-on-the-Lake	Headington
New York	Ontario, Canada	Oxford OX3 7AD
N.Y. 10118	L0S 1J0	United Kingdom

Cataloguing in Publication Data
Kalman, Bobbie, 1947-
  I am a part of nature

(The Primary Ecology Series)
Includes index.
ISBN 0-86505-552-1 (library bound) ISBN 0-86505-578-5 (pbk.)

1. Ecology - Juvenile literature.
2. Man - Influence on nature - Juvenile literature.
3. Natural history - Juvenile literature.
I. Schaub, Janine. II. Title. III. Series

QH541.14.K35 1992   j574.5

Contents

(above) All life comes from the sun. Without the sun's warmth and energy, no living thing would survive. (below) We are connected to insects, plants, animals, and people. How are these things important parts of our lives?

What is nature?

What does the word "nature" mean to you? Does a camping trip or a walk in the woods pop into your mind when you think of nature? Is nature the birds, animals, forests, and fields that surround you? Nature is all these things, but it is much more.

Part of the living world

Being a part of nature means being a part of the living world. Each person is connected to the air, water, and land. We are linked to animals and plants with which we share the earth. We breathe the air, drink the water, and eat the food that comes from plants and animals. Without these things, we would not be alive.

Indoor beings

It is sometimes hard to think of ourselves as being a part of nature. Many of us live in cities and spend much of our time indoors. The toys, furniture, and other objects in our homes have been made by people. These things do not make us feel close to nature. In fact, they make us feel as if we are a part of a human-made world. Watching television, eating packaged foods, and traveling in cars and buses are all activities that separate us from the natural world.

Discovering our connections

We need to think about our connections to the living world. Once we begin to understand how we are joined to the natural things around us, we will start to feel that we are a part of nature and that nature is a part of us.

We are connected to nature through the food we eat, the water we drink, and the air we breathe.

Human beings are a natural part of the earth just as plants and animals are. Marc is demonstrating this fact!

We are all members of a large family of plants, animals, and people that share the earth.

Part of a big family

You are an important member of your family. You, your parents, and your brothers and sisters all work together to create a special relationship. You are also a member of the large family of plants and animals living on Planet Earth. Every creature, including you, adds something special to this family.

Respecting our home

The house or apartment in which we live is not our only home. People, plants, and animals also share another, much bigger home—our earth. The natural world around us belongs to every living creature on our planet. This big home must remain a clean and safe place for all living beings because we have no other place to live.

A "natural" discovery

The story on the following pages shows how one young person discovered that she was very much part of the natural world. Do you have a similar story?

I am a part of nature

It was the last weekend of summer. It felt as if I had explored everything there was to explore in the forest and swamp near our family cabin. With the start of a new school year only three days away, there seemed to be nothing left to do but sit by the swamp and watch the sun go down—and swat mosquitoes.

Many times that summer I had allowed one of those annoying bugs to land and push its needly nose into my arm. I would let it feed until it was fat and then I'd swat it—splat! But that day, sitting alone in the late afternoon sun, I became fascinated by the bug that was biting me.

I watched her abdomen swell up with my blood, like a tiny red light bulb, and it suddenly occurred to me that this little creature was about to fly away with a little bit of **me** inside her. I had become a part of her, so I decided to let her go on her way. She lifted off, flying low across the water.

My attention was just drifting back to the sun's warmth when I spotted a familiar sight. There, just a short distance from me, was an enormous bullfrog. "Boy, he's big!" I thought and made up my mind to catch him, when I noticed the mosquito that had bitten me was buzzing right towards him. In a flash of a tongue, she, with that little bit of me, vanished inside the frog's mouth. "Hey!" I said out loud, "Now I'm part of a frog!" That was even more exciting than being part of a bug!

Moments later a big, black water snake slid into the swamp water. It headed straight for the bullfrog that contained a part of me. The huge frog's legs thrashed as the snake struck. The frog and snake twisted about in the dark water until the snake swam off, victorious. I felt as if I was a part of their struggle, and the snake got to take a part of me home!

As the fiery red sun went down behind the maples, I slowly walked back to the cabin, wondering about being part of all the things around me. If the mosquito had survived to lay her eggs, then each one would have had a piece of me in it. And when they hatched, they would have spread out all over the forest taking me with them to become parts of birds, dragonflies, and bats. Pretty soon, I would have been part of the entire forest! I felt a wonderful sense of belonging to all things.

But all my good feelings about belonging to the forest changed the very next day. My big brother returned from a trip into town and brought me a surprise—a real bow-and-arrow set.

All morning I practiced my aim on a target in front of the cabin. In the afternoon, I set out into the woods.

Carrying the bow and arrows filled me with new feelings. I was being trusted with a powerful weapon. I realized that the bow was strong and the arrows sharp. If I were hunting to feed myself, I could kill a squirrel, a groundhog, or even a deer. Being a part of bugs, frogs, and snakes seemed unimportant compared to the feeling of being a powerful hunter!

A little before sunset, I found myself stalking through the woods near the swamp, and a movement in a big maple tree froze me. Could it be a squirrel or a raccoon?

I stalked closer. The creature had not moved again, so I was unable to recognize its shape in the fading light. I was so excited, I decided to shoot. "I probably won't hit it anyway," I reasoned. I drew the arrow back to my ear and let it fly.

A moment later my arrow hit its mark and something tumbled over and over and fell with a "thump!" to the ground. I ran to where it lay. There, beside the trunk of the maple, I found a great horned owl with huge yellow eyes. It was the magical and mysterious bird I had only before seen in photographs.

Looking at the dead owl made me shiver and feel frightened. It was so beautiful, and I had killed it! Suddenly, I felt totally unwelcome in the forest where only yesterday I had felt so much at home. I couldn't think of anything to do but bury the owl. I found a stick and made a hole in the ground. I buried the owl in the shallow pit and thought about the waiting bugs and worms that would make the owl become part of the soil.

Just about to leave, I glanced up to where the owl had been perched and noticed something hanging there. It was a black water snake! It was the same snake that had eaten the bullfrog because it still had a bulge in its middle. The owl had been eating the snake when I shot it with my arrow.

I was horrified to realize that I had killed an owl! Somehow, without tripping, I ran through the dark woods to the cabin.

Late that fall, we returned to our cabin. I ran to the swamp as soon as we arrived. I found the owl's grave by spotting the digging stick I had used to make the hole.

As I stared, I realized I had buried the owl beside a blueberry bush. Now the owl was part of that bush. Surprisingly, for that time of year, there were still a few berries on the branches. I picked two of the plumpest ones, popped them into my mouth, and found that they were sweet and full of juice. I realized that these were **my** berries—mine and the owl's, the snake's, the frog's, and the mosquito's, too. The feeling of belonging to the forest came back, and I felt forgiven and welcome once again.

Questions for discussion

• How does the story "I am a part of nature" illustrate that human beings are connected to other living things?

• Can you think of how plants and animals are a part of human beings?

• The story shows a forest food chain. One living thing eats another and is, in turn, eaten by another creature. Are human beings parts of food chains? How is death a part of life in the food chain?

• Why does the child in the story kill the owl? Why does she later feel forgiven?

Food chains and webs

In order to grow, every living thing in nature needs nourishment. Plants receive their energy from water, air, and sunshine. Every time an animal eats, it also takes in food energy. When a berry is eaten by a bird, and the bird is eaten by a fox, energy is passed along a **food chain**. People are a part of food chains, too. Most of us eat both plants and animals. Some animals belong to several food chains. Food chains that connect form a **food web**.

The snake is about to eat the butterfly. Later, that same snake might be eaten by an owl.

With a roll of string, these students are demonstrating how food webs work. Each child is a plant, animal, or decomposer. The string is passed from the sun, who is in the center, to a plant and to several animals that eat that plant. From those animals, the string continues to animals that eat the first animals and then to decomposers that break down dead animals, which then nourish new plants. The string-web demonstration allows you to experience how animals, plants, and decomposers are connected in a real food web. Try it. It's fun!

The forest recycling game

Decomposers, such as beetles and earthworms, are also a part of food chains and food webs. They help break down dead plants and animals and return the nourishment of the food chain back to the soil. Nothing is wasted in nature! This game shows how decomposers are a necessary part of food chains and webs.

You need:
- Ten or more children
- A gymnasium or school yard
- Paper bags for 6 players and at least 60 markers

How to play the game:

1) Roles are assigned to the players as follows: There will be six mice, two owls, and two decomposers—one worm and one maggot or slug.

2) The decomposers scatter the markers about the playing area. The markers represent seeds and other nutrient sources for the forest mice.

3) Each mouse is given a paper bag, which is its "stomach." When given the signal, the mice run around putting nutrients into their stomachs.

4) On a signal from the leader, the owls fly out to catch the mice. (They tag them with one hand.) When an owl catches a mouse, the mouse passes on the nutrients it has gathered to the owl. The owl takes the bag and flies off to catch more mice. The dead mouse leaves the game.

5) When all the mice have been caught, the "dead" mice become "owl catchers." Owl catchers can be predators (such as a lynx), diseases, or old age that kills the birds. When the owl catchers tag the owls, the owls must drop the bags they have collected. Now the worms and other decomposers go into action by taking all the nutrients and scattering them about the forest again. The game can keep going indefinitely, just as energy continues along a food chain.

To make the game more fun, these students made mouse ears and whiskers, insect antennae, and owl feathers and wore them when they played the game. They used popsicle sticks as markers, but you can also use marbles or jellybeans.

What is a life cycle?

Life is a series of **cycles**. Water, air, soil, and all living things have cycles and are parts of cycles. You experience the seasons of the year—spring, summer, fall, and winter. They, too, form a cycle. Once winter has finished, spring comes again, and the cycle of the seasons continues. Each year you start a new grade at school and have another birthday. Each year you begin a new cycle.

Life can be called a cycle, too. Living creatures, such as the tiny birds in the picture above, are born, grow old, and die. Every living thing goes through this same cycle of changes. Some living things have long life cycles. Trees, for example, can live for hundreds of years. Other living creatures, such as house flies, have very short life cycles of just a few months.

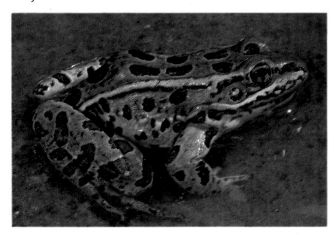

The leopard frog is born, becomes a tadpole, turns into a frog, and lays eggs that hatch into tadpoles. Later, the leopard frog dies. Its body breaks down and helps a water lily grow.

14

A frog's life cycle

The leopard frog in this drawing started its life cycle as an egg. It grew into a tadpole with a tail and swam busily around its pond. After two or three months, it developed front and back limbs and changed into a frog.

When the weather turned cold, the leopard frog burrowed into the mud at the bottom of the pond to wait out the winter. At the first sign of spring, it dug itself out and started looking for juicy bugs to fill its empty stomach.

One year, however, the leopard frog did not come out of its burrow. It was old, and the cycle of its life was over. Slowly, the frog's body **decayed**, or broke down. It released **nutrients** into the mud at the bottom of the pond. Nutrients are food materials that nourish living things.

The next spring, a new lily pad started to grow in the very spot where the frog died. The lily pad used the foods in the mud left behind by the frog's body to start its own life cycle.

Nothing comes, nothing leaves

Nothing has been added or lost from our planet since it was first formed. Everything is used again in one form or another. The air, water, and land have been around for millions of years. Living things die, become part of the soil, and give life to new plants. The earth recycles everything.

Think about how you, too, are a part of our earth when you perform these actions:

1. Take a sip from a glass of water. Swirl it around your mouth for a minute. That same sip may have been drunk by a caveman!

2. Rub a few grains of dirt between your fingers. You could be pinching the dust remains of a dinosaur!

3. Hold your breath for a few seconds. The air in your lungs may have filled the lungs of an ancient Egyptian!

4. Visualize a landfill site full of human-made objects. Although these objects originally came from natural materials, these materials were changed into forms that are no longer natural. Many human-made objects such as plastic do not break down and become part of the earth again. They cannot become a part of living things in the future, and they cannot leave the earth. They just pile up. When we create these objects, we also use up many natural resources that cannot be replaced. List ten ways we can save natural resources and reduce the amount of garbage we create.

A bit of nature every day

Remind yourself that you are a part of nature by making it a part of your everyday life. Set up a miniature environment inside or outside your home or school so you can observe and take part in the daily activities of other living things. Use the suggestions on these two pages.

(above) The students in this class feed their lunch leftovers to worms. (left) This student made her own bird feeder. (below left) A large terrarium was set up in the library of this school. Students take turns looking after the tiny garden. (below right) Students collected feathers they found on the way to and from school until they completely dressed this naked bird!

Setting up a worm bin

Set up a worm bin and start composting your family or school lunchroom food scraps. When people compost with worms, it is called **vermi-composting**. Vermi-composting reduces the amount of garbage your family throws away and, at the same time, allows you to have fun watching wiggly worms!

A terrarium

Get a large glass jar from a restaurant or a bulk-food store or use an old aquarium. Put a layer of gravel and then a layer of potting soil in the bottom and plant several kinds of tropical plants. Find out which plants will grow best in a terrarium. Use a spray bottle to keep your tiny jungle moist at all times. Place your terrarium in a sunny spot and enjoy watching your "rainforest-in-miniature" grow!

Front-row seats!

With the help of an adult, make or buy a bird feeder. Sit quietly outside or in front of the window nearest the feeder and watch the birds visit it. Be sure to keep the feeder filled so that the birds that come to depend on the seeds you put out will not go hungry.

Watching eggs hatch

Ask your teacher if your class could watch baby chicks hatch from eggs. It is an exciting experience to see these tiny birds burst out of their eggshells. Did you know that you, also, started out as an egg?

In winter, you might discover a tree trunk hidden under snow. In summer, you might see a pair of praying mantises that are about to have a battle!

Fine-tune your senses

Have you ever been on a wilderness adventure? The most important tools to take along on such a nature hike are your finely tuned senses. Smelling, touching, tasting, hearing, and seeing the world around you is the best way to discover nature.

Alone with nature

Choose a spot where you feel comfortable. Sit quietly by yourself and close your eyes. Feel your mind become silent and your body relax. With your eyes closed, listen to and smell the world around you. Now, open your eyes and see what you have heard and smelled. Without saying or

writing anything, think about how you are a part of nature.

Notice the sights and colors around you. Observe any movement on the ground and in the trees or sky. Listen for the chirps of birds or the "peeps" of a spring peeper frog!

Ready for discovery

Before going on a nature walk, it is important to know a little bit about the area to which you are going and the weather conditions forecasted for the day of your visit. Dressing properly will allow you to have a more enjoyable time outdoors.

Tools that may enrich your nature walk are a magnifying glass, a camera, binoculars, a compass, and a sketch pad. These objects will help you make a careful study of your surroundings, both close up and far away.

When going on a nature walk, use all your senses and look in every direction. Be careful not to disturb any creatures!

Your natural home

When you are hiking in a wilderness area, think of the trip as a journey through your own home. As you are walking over grasses and past trees and bushes, pretend that these natural surroundings are your floors, walls, and furniture.

Imagine that you and the thousands of fellow creatures that make this area their home are your family. You are all depending on one another for survival. If you visit a natural area thinking these thoughts, you will find yourself walking more carefully than you have ever walked before!

Nature-hike guidelines

On any hike through a natural area, it is important to show respect by leaving the surroundings as undisturbed as possible. The following list is a good guideline for your next nature hike:

1. Do not take any samples. You may be disturbing nature's balance by removing a part of a creature's home or dinner.

2. If you are walking through a bushy area, gently push plants aside as you walk past. Never break branches, strip bark, or carve into a living tree. These actions will injure the tree and might cause it to die.

3. Walk quietly and avoid talking loudly. If you keep noise to a minimum, you will not frighten other creatures, and you will have a greater chance of seeing wildlife.

4. If you see some garbage left behind by others, pick it up and take it out of the wilderness area.

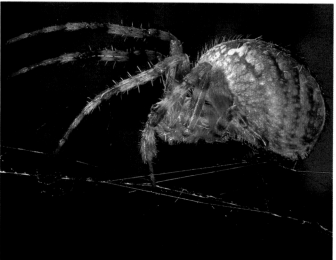

You might see these things!

If you are very quiet on your nature walk, you might be lucky enough to see some of nature's treasures shown on these two pages. Which of these natural wonders have you observed up close? Have you ever seen: a deer mouse

peeking out of its den; a hungry baby bird; a spider busy spinning a web; a polythemus moth with "eyes" on its wings; a rabbit looking around for food; a thistle seed caught by the wind? What wonderful sights have you discovered in the wild?

Nature fun

A theme walk

Think of a theme for your next nature walk. A **theme**, or subject, for your walk could be "an ankle-view of the world." Concentrating on your theme, you would pay special attention to the plants and animals next to the ground. Theme walks may help you see, hear, and smell plants and animals that you may have missed otherwise.

A silent walk

Go on a silent nature walk with a group of friends. Use your finely tuned senses to observe the sights and sounds around you. Think about how the plants and animals you see are connected to one another. How are they connected to you?

Notice the negative spaces on your walk. Negative spaces can be bare ground in a field of grass or snow, a patch of sky between trees, or even total silence. Why are negative spaces an important part of your experience?

When you want to share an experience with the others in your group, raise your hand and point, but do not speak. Allow your friends to experience what they see in their own special ways.

After the walk is over, talk about what you have observed and compare your impressions with those of your friends. Did each of you see the same things in the same ways? Discuss the value of silent observation. How does it help you learn about and appreciate nature?

These kids discovered some tiny flowers and three little marmots on their silent walk.

A wilderness treasure hunt

With a group of friends, make a list or draw pictures of plants, leaves, seeds, cones, animals, butterflies, insects, and flowers you might see on a nature walk. Give each person in the group a copy of the list and set off on your treasure hunt. Tick off each item you see and briefly describe its size, color, how it smells, or how it moves.

A mystery animal

Create a mystery and ask your friends to solve it. Write a story about an animal of your choice and give your friends just enough clues to help them identify it. Describe your creature's habitat, giving lots of details about sights, sounds, and smells. What is the creature's place in the food chain?

The students in the bottom picture demonstrate that when the population of human beings or animals grows, there is less food and shelter for wild creatures. Three children stand on one side of the leader (they are deer); fifteen to twenty stand on the other (they are the habitat of the deer). The two groups face away from one another, and each player chooses one of three symbols: shelter (hands steepled over head), water (hands over mouth), food (hands over stomach). The deer walk over to the habitat players and choose one player with a matching symbol. The six players now go to the other side. With backs turned, new symbols are chosen. Soon the deer side (population) becomes large, and the habitat side (food, water, shelter) becomes very small.

How many pictured items have you found?

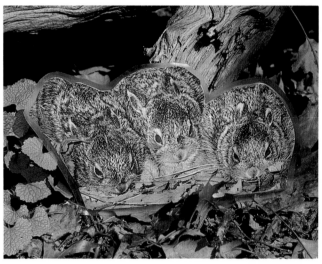

Hide a picture of a plant or animal along a nature trail and challenge your friends to find it. Make sure it is well camouflaged!

The game described in the paragraph on the left and shown above is called "Oh, deer!"

27

Gaia, the living planet

Some scientists describe the Planet Earth as a large living body because it is the only planet in our solar system that has the right ingredients to keep things alive. Its temperature is neither too hot nor too cold; the amount of oxygen in its air is right for breathing.

Those who believe that the earth is a living planet call it Gaia after a Greek goddess of long ago. Gaia's living power is a part of plants, animals, and people. It passes through the air, water, and soil. Everything that is a part of earth is a part of Gaia!

Water, air, soil, mountains, plants, and animals are all parts of Gaia's "body." All these things help Gaia remain in balance. They provide the right formula for life on the Planet Earth. What can people do to make sure Gaia stays alive?

Gaia is alive!

The sun warms my face
as I walk across the living land.
Strong and firm,
Gaia supports my footsteps.
She anchors the majestic trees that give
me shade and clean the air I breathe.
She gives life to plants and animals.
Generous with her gifts, she feeds me.
Her soil has been enriched from things
that have died and returned to it—
for dead things nourish the living.

Gaia is alive!
She is the surf that crashes against the
shore and withdraws again.
She is the air, she is the sea, she is the
creatures that swim, crawl, and fly.
She is the delicate aroma of a gentle
flower and the breathtaking colors of a
beautiful sunset.

I live in a world that is made
of concrete and bricks.
My human-made environment
often makes me forget
that I am a part of nature.
The earth does not belong to me:
I belong to it—
for a very short time.
The sun warms my face
For I, too, am Gaia.

The living planet was named after a Greek goddess of long ago whose name was Gaia.

Some parts of Gaia play a very important role in keeping the rest of the planet alive. Rainforests, for example, are essential to the earth. We must work hard to make sure that they are saved. They are necessary for the survival of all life on earth!

A great, big challenge

If we think of ourselves as living beings who are a part of a living planet, we will feel more connected to the environment. We will understand that keeping the natural world clean will keep us healthy. The challenge for us today is to live in harmony with one another and with the living world and feel proud that we are doing our best to care for our planet.

A nature-friendly attitude

Caring for the earth is a big job. Sometimes it seems like such a huge task that we do not know where to begin. Even though we may care for the earth, we pollute and damage it in many ways. A first step towards change is developing a new, nature-friendly attitude. This new attitude means making sensible choices about how to live without hurting the earth.

Nature-friendly decisions

Everyone makes decisions that affect the environment. What nature-friendly decisions can you and your friends make when faced with these choices?

1. You live a short distance from school, but your mother often drives you there and home.

2. Your family has several trinkets made from ivory. You know that an elephant had to die so these types of objects could be made. You also have other objects in your home that came from endangered plants and animals.

3. You and your family throw out food leftovers with your garbage.

4. You spend twenty minutes in the shower each morning and run water while you brush your teeth.

Shout out loud!

With a group of friends, discuss these and other "nature-unfriendly" situations and come up with a positive-action plan. Share your plan with others and convince them also to adopt a nature-friendly attitude. If you love the earth, you will treat plants and animals with great care. Remember! You are a part of nature and nature is a part of you!

Olivia is showing fruit made of ebony and ivory. Ebony is a hardwood that comes from very old, endangered rainforest trees. Ivory comes from elephant tusks. Why should you not buy objects made from ebony or ivory?

Remind yourselves that you belong to the living planet by shouting out loud, "I am a part of nature!"

Glossary

burrow A hole dug in the ground by an animal in which it lives and hides

camouflage An appearance or behavior that conceals an animal from its natural enemies

composting Putting leftover foods and plant matter in a special pile and letting it decay

connection A link

cycle A series of events that occurs again and again in a certain order

decay To rot

decomposer Something that causes something to decay or rot

ebony A hard, black wood that comes from endangered rainforest trees

endangered In danger of not surviving

energy The power needed to do something

enrich To improve

environment The surroundings in which plants, animals, or people live

food chain A series of events in which food energy is passed as one creature eats another

food web Many connected food chains

landfill site A place where garbage is buried under and on top of layers of dirt

nutrient A nutritious substance needed by the body

predator An animal that eats another animal

rainforest A forest found in a tropical area where there is a lot of rain

recycle To make something useful again

relationship The condition of being connected

survival The state of remaining alive

terrarium A small container used for growing plants or as an environment for small land animals such as lizards

vermi-composting Allowing worms to break down garbage in a bin

wilderness A wild place where no people live

2 3 4 5 6 7 8 9 0 Printed in USA 1 0 9 8 7 6 5 4 3

Index